D0116408

THE TOUCH BOOK

by Jane Belk Moncure
illustrated by
Lois Axeman
created by The Child's World

 CHILDRENS PRESS ™

CHICAGO

Cover and Title Page
Designed by Dolores Hollister

Library of Congress Cataloging in Publication Data

Moncure, Jane Belk.
  The Touch Book.

  (The Five senses)
  Summary: Fingers are made for touching
fuzzy, cold, warm, sticky, lumpy, furry,
rough, smooth, soft, hard, slippery, and
prickly things.
    1. Touch—Juvenile literature. [1. Touch.
2. Fingers] I. Axeman, Lois, ill. II. Title.
III. Series: Moncure, Jane Belk. Five senses.
QP451.M7   152.1'82   82-4154
ISBN 0-516-03254-2   AACR2

THE
TOUCH
BOOK

Fingers are for touching
fuzzy things
like pussywillows

and baby ducklings,

dandelion seeds
that float in the wind,

and caterpillars
that curl up into tiny balls.

Fingers are for touching
cold things
like snowflakes,
and warm things
like a cup of hot chocolate.

Fingers are for touching
sticky things like glue
when you're making valentines,

strawberry jam when
you're making a sandwich,

or cotton candy
when you're at the zoo.

Fingers are for touching
lumpy things like clay
that squeezes into balls

and mud that squishes
into lumpy mud pies
that dry in the sun.

Fingers are for touching
furry things like a lamb
at the fair

or kittens in a basket.

Fingers are for touching
rough things like sandpaper,

the bark
on a tree,

or tiny bits of shells
at the beach.

Fingers are for touching
smooth things
like rose petals

and silk ribbons,

or stones
you can skip
in the pond.

Fingers are for touching
soft things
like dough you roll into balls
before making cookies.

Fingers are for touching
hard things like the floor

when you do a cartwheel,

or a big rock
when you're sitting on it.

Fingers are for touching
slippery things like soap
in your bath,

gelatin squares
for dessert,

or raindrops that slide
down the windowpane.

Fingers are for touching
prickly things like cockleburs

and pine cones.

Sometimes you touch
with one finger.

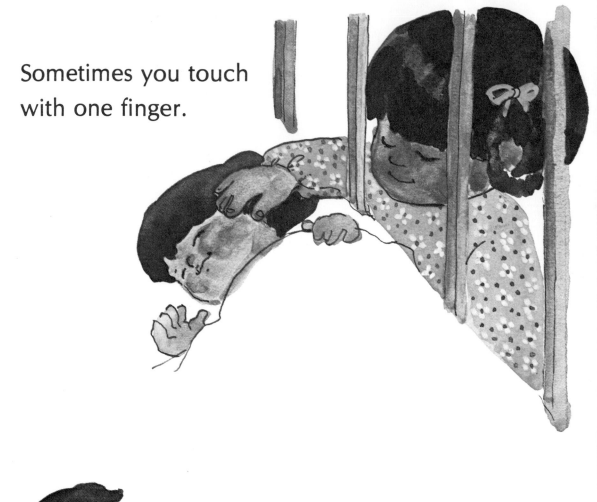

Sometimes you touch
with your nose.

Sometimes you touch
with your cheek.

Sometimes you touch
with your toes.

Sometimes you reach out
with both arms

to touch someone
who needs you.

Sometimes,
the best kind of touching
is hugging!